彩梦世界

(英汉对照)

〔加拿大〕布迈恪/著　金圣华/译

商务印书馆
2008年·北京

目 录

001　序一：有生命的颜色　林青霞
005　序二：寻找彩梦世界　金圣华

众彩缤纷

002　Olympic Colours
003　华光溢彩迎奥运
004　Rainbow
005　彩虹
006　插图

绿色系列

Colours of the River	008
河流之色	009
Colours of the Wood	010
森林之色	011
Green 1	012
绿之一	013
Green 2	014
绿之二	015
Green Shadows	016
绿影	017
Green Mist	018
绿雾	019
Green Resonance	020
绿色共鸣	021

Philodendron	022
蔓	023
插图	024

蓝色系列

026	Blue
027	蓝
028	Peacock Blue
029	孔雀蓝
030	Blue Evening
031	蓝暮
032	Ultramarine
033	佛青色
034	Prussian Blue
035	普鲁士蓝
036	Indigo
037	靛蓝
038	Cobalt Blue
039	钴蓝
040	Pale Blue
041	浅蓝
042	插图

紫色系列

Lilac	044
紫丁香	045
Mauve	046

浅紫	047
Pale Mauve	048
淡紫	049
Purple	050
紫	051
Purple Flower	052
紫花	053
Night's Purple	054
夜紫	055
Purple Shadow	056
紫影	057
Purple Poppies	058
紫罂粟	059
Purple Petals Fall	060
紫瓣飘落	061
A Flood of Purple	062
紫潮	063
Purple the Warrior	064
紫色战士	065
插图	066

紫红系列

068	Magenta 1
069	紫红之一
070	Magenta 2
071	紫红之二
072	Fuchsia
073	洋红
074	插图

银灰系列

Grey	076
灰	077
Dove Grey	078
鸽灰	079
Silver	080
银	081
Snow	082
雪	083
White	084
白	085
插图	086

黄色系列

088	Yellow 1
089	黄之一
090	Yellow 2
091	黄之二
092	The Shadow of Yellow
093	黄影
094	Lemon Yellow
095	柠檬黄
096	The Dream of Yellow
097	黄之梦
098	Orange
099	橙
100	Copper
101	铜

102	Brown
103	棕色
104	插图

红色系列

Red 1	106
红之一	107
Red 2	108
红之二	109
Pink 1	110
粉红之一	111
Pink 2	112
粉红之二	113
Pink Doll	114
粉红娃娃	115
插图	116

黑色系列

118	Black 1
119	黑之一
120	Black 2
121	黑之二
122	Black 3
123	黑之三
124	Black 4
125	黑之四

126	Black Dot
127	黑点
128	Black and Red
129	黑与红
130	Black and Green
131	黑与绿
132	Black and Purple
133	黑与紫
134	Black and Mauve
135	黑与浅紫
136	插图

瑰色灿烂

The Colours of the Roses	138
玫瑰之色	139
插图	140

| 作者简介 | 141 |
| 译者简介 | 143 |

序 一

有生命的颜色

林青霞

金圣华教授一身枣红出现在我家前院,高雅中透着风韵。枣红穿在我身上,从来没好看过。这颜色经过金教授深浅得宜的搭配,煞是好看。这是她给我的第一个印象,因此每当我想起她,脑子里就浮起红酒的颜色。

由于我对文学的喜爱和渴望在英文程度上有所增进,朋友把当时在中文大学教翻译、现在又是翻译学会会长的她介绍给我。她即使非常的忙碌,仍然抽出时间,在每个星期六的下午,带着她翻译的文章到我家,很有耐心的指导我。我称呼她金教授,但她坚持要我直呼她的名字,这样更增加了亲切感,我们的友谊也从此开始。

沙士期间我去了一趟美国,因此我们有很长一段时间没有见面。回港后,我们有时会在星期六的下午,相约在半岛酒店喝下午茶。在那儿我们谈文学、谈哲学、谈艺术。间或也会到对面的艺术中心看画,消磨着很有意义的下午。在交谈的过程中圣华给了我很多启发和灵感。

有一次我们谈到颜色,她很兴奋地告诉我,有几本是专门讲颜色的书,每一种颜色都有一本。后来我们在台北的诚品书店找到了。我买了两套,有红色、蓝色、紫色、白色和黑色,一人一套,我们各自捧着自己的书,像小孩子捧着心爱的玩具,欢天喜地地回家。

向来对颜色没有深刻研究的我,圣华问起来,才开始思考这个问题。

小时候很喜欢鲜黄色,之后有很长一段时间对颜色没什么特别感觉,好像也无所谓,后来发觉心情不好的时候喜欢穿灰色,有时会穿黑色,因为黑色最安全,最不容易出错。经常买红色的衣服但很少穿。最近钟情于象牙色也喜欢粉紫和dirty pink(暗粉红),也许是反应出我目前的心境吧。

很高兴看到圣华翻释的一本有关颜色的诗集——《彩梦世界》,让我对色彩有了新奇微妙的感受。

很喜欢这首"紫瓣飘落"
紫瓣飘落于
静止的湖上
湖水哭泣
为一张逝去的脸庞
那脸永不会再次
映照于湖面

紫瓣飘浮于
静谧的空中
宛如音乐

几片紫瓣,竟是这样空灵而美丽,真叫人感动。这使我想起,有一次我和圣华到香港艺术中心看完画,她一身紫色纱裙,由石阶上走下。我迎着她的手,那衣裙在风中摆动,真是宛如音乐,好美。

另一首"黑与绿"
窥进黑黝黝的池塘
我瞧见一张脸庞
给涟漪弄皱
受绿苇纠缠
让黑色水鸟穿梭划过

这脸是我的
你的,还是一个陌生人的?

用黑来形容池水的深沉和静谧,用绿苇形容纠缠的感情。因为黑和绿的结合而产生不同的面貌。记得有一次我和圣华见面,两人不约而同的都穿黑配绿的衣服,也都穿出各自的味道,两人相视而笑,非常有趣。

"红之一"
红在我头颅里尖叫
以利爪抓住我的脑
它那红宝的眼睛
窥入
本来永不该瞥的地方

红会尖叫,红有利爪,红还会窥视,真叫人震惊,原来红这么有生命力。

不知道为什么,我总喜欢买红色的衣服和红色的唇膏,却很少用也很少穿，看了这首诗，才让我意识到，原来我喜欢的是它那令人惊艳的特色和生命力。

圣华喜欢美丽的颜色，她能读出加拿大著名诗人布迈恪的内心世界，诠译出以颜色为主题的美妙诗句。透过她的译作，我发现，颜色不只是形容词，它也可以是动词和名词，不只代表静止的色素，它也有动感，甚至充满着生命力。

诗人布迈恪的创作，加上圣华翻译的"创作"，不只诱发视觉，而且可以唤起听觉和嗅觉，让我们的生命、我们的世界增添了梦幻的色彩。这个世界真美妙。

林青霞

2008年5月2日

序 二

寻找彩梦世界

金圣华

从小,就喜欢做梦。

长大后,依然喜欢做梦。夜里,沉睡时做梦,将醒未醒时,也做梦。白天,听不进枯燥沉闷的演讲时,思想飞得老远,海阔天空,自由翱翔;看不惯虚假冷漠的脸孔时,虽身困室中,也会神游物外;而每当失意沮丧时,更努力追梦,寻梦,希望把灰暗的现实,化为绚丽的梦境。

谁说,梦是没有颜色的?对我来说,所有的梦,夜里的,白天的,梦境也罢,梦想也罢,都是灿烂多姿的,能使平凡素淡的人生,添上一抹抹缤纷斑斓的色彩。

2007年5月,从香港来到北京,观赏白先勇《青春版牡丹亭》第一百场演出,一踏出机场,就看到迎面而来的奥运标语——同一个世界,同一个梦想 (One World, One Dream)。好一个世界大同、万邦协和的理念！不错，这世上，的确应该消除歧见，打破隔阂，为全人类的福祉而同心协力，实现梦想。然而这个人类共同的梦，究竟是怎么样的？我想，应该是异中求同，而非单调统一的，换言之，这个梦不是黑白之梦，而是五光十色而又融洽和谐，多姿多彩而又欣悦怡人的，因此，这世界也将因梦境的实现而变成一个包括各色人种、包含各种宗教、包容各类思想的大同世界，而这个"One Dream"当然就是一个充满生机、充满希望的彩色之梦了。

2003年，加拿大名诗人布迈恪（Michael Bullock）出版了以 Colours 为名的诗集，随即寄赠给我，并问我是否有意将之译成中文。我当时因为公事繁多，且正为筹办"新纪元全球华文青年文学奖"而忙得不可开交，于是就把这项好友托付的任务搁下了。事隔数年，在北京街头瞥见奥运的标语后，"世界"、"梦想"等字眼，一直在心中萦绕不散，回港后再次细读布迈恪的 Colours，发现这本以色彩为名、以色彩为主的集子，字里行间，充满了梦与幻、光与影、虚与实、回忆与追思、憧憬与向往的诗情和画意。这是一本不折不扣描绘彩梦世界的奇幻之作，如能在2008年出版，亦可在欢庆奥运的气氛中，为书林译海增添一些色彩，这就是本书中译的缘起与由来。

布迈恪原籍英国，后移居加拿大，为著名诗人、画家、小说家、剧作家及翻译家，于1918年出生于伦敦，年轻时曾进美术学校习画，课余从事写作及翻译。1968年以英联邦学人身份，访问加拿大英属哥伦比亚大学，1966年以麦克谷菲访问英语教授身份访问美国俄亥俄大学。1969年底，重返英属哥伦比亚大学，出任创作系主任，主讲翻译课。1983年，以终身教授（Professor Emeritus）身份从该校荣休。退休后，布迈恪创作不辍，翻译不断，迄今出版的诗集及小说逾五十种，剧本两种，译自德、法、意文学作品约两百种,其作品已翻译成多种欧洲及东方语言,包括中、日、韩、印等文,其中尤以中文译作数量最丰。

1974年春,我趁长假之便,远赴加拿大英属哥伦比亚大学创作系进修,有幸结识布迈恪教授,自此展开一段长逾三十年的友谊。我不但从布迈恪身上学习了不少教授翻译的良方,也成为介绍布氏作品的主要译者,先后翻译过他的诗集《石与影》(*Stone and Shadow*)及小说《黑娃的故事》(*The Story of Noire*),并在国内出版。

翻译布迈恪的作品,每每是一种苦乐参半、惊喜交集的经历,原因是他的作品看似简单,实则艰难,在翻译的过程中,常使译者感到殚精竭虑,力不从心。布氏是超现实主义大师,不论是诗、是画,或是小说、戏剧,他的作品总带有一种洒脱不羁、恣意奔放,然而又深沉奥秘、难以尽窥的特色,因此,译者往往会在字句的表面结构与深层意义中彷徨失措,举棋不定,而真正尝透了"迷失译途"(Lost in Translation)的况味。

布迈恪的《彩梦世界》是一本另辟蹊径的力作。在诗人长逾七十载的创作生涯中,色彩一直是不可或缺的文学元素。根据诗人自述,最初的诗作,是一首很像俳句的小诗,一共只有两行:"月亮是一朵黄色的玫瑰／飘泛于穹苍的紫川",自此之后,这紫黄二色,就不时出现在布氏的作品中,不论是诗,是画,往往双色并呈,互相衬托。其实,在诗品中以色彩写景,以色彩绘物,以色彩烘托气氛,原是不论中外文学中共有的手法,不足为奇。以中国诗词为例,如"万丈红泉落,迢迢半紫氛"(张九龄《湖口望庐山瀑布水》),"红酥手,黄藤酒,满城春色宫墙柳"(陆游《钗头凤》),"江南好,风景旧曾谙,日出江花红胜火,春来江水绿如蓝。能不忆江南"(白居易《忆江南》），"红树青山日欲斜，长郊草色绿无涯"（欧阳修《丰乐亭游春》），"和露摘黄花，带霜烹紫蟹，煮酒烧红叶"（马致远《夜行船·秋思》）等等，莫不把色彩当作形容词，来描绘实物实景，使笔下形象更添姿彩。又如"春风又绿江南岸"（王安石《泊船瓜州》），则把色彩当作动词用。诗人布迈恪多年来一直采用以色彩为形容词的传统手法，偶尔也会将色彩当作动词或副词来用。

自2000年起，布迈恪不但开始把色彩当作一个名词，而且当作一个与实物无涉的主体来看待。他尝试把色彩拟人化，写了一首有关《红》的诗，自此之后，灵感源源不绝，创作了大量有关色彩的诗作，并汇编成集，名之曰*Colours*。

在这些诗中，布迈恪追随法国诗人蓝波（Rimbaud 1854-1891）的足迹，采取了模拟"综合感官知觉"（synaesthesia）的手法。这种手法简述之，即为各感官之间的交互作用。视听联觉者可在聆听的同时，通过联感，看见某物的色彩。诗人运用一种类似的联想法，看见某一种色彩时，马上在脑海中浮现出某个声音、某缕气息或某种思绪，因而激发起赋诗的灵感，创作出许多情景交融、声色俱全的作品。自此，每一色彩已化为本身含有特殊意义的实体，内蕴丰富而寓意深刻。

如何把布迈恪幻彩作品的神韵，充分再现在译文中？首先，布迈恪这一系列色彩之作，是一种崭新的尝试，不但与中国古典的诗词迥异，与英诗的传统也不尽相同。对布氏来说，颜色如梦如幻，可敬可友，通过各种色彩浓淡深浅的描述，他把内心深处的喜、怒、哀、乐，恐惧与期盼、失落与希冀、追忆与憧憬、冲突与协调等等，都刻画得丝丝入扣，而又往往出人意表。

一般来说，颜色是与思想情绪直接联系的，就以奥运旗帜上的五环为例吧！这五环以白色为背景，分别为蓝、黄、黑、红、绿共五色（图案设计于1913年，正式采用于1920年在比利时安特卫普（Antwerp）举行的奥运会上），彩色之圈，环环相扣，代表寰宇五大洲由奥运精神联为一体，融洽无间。通常，黑色代表尊严高贵，白色代表纯洁优雅，红色代表热情华丽，绿色代表青春，蓝色代表平和，黄色代表活泼，但是这种种联想，却常因时因地、因人因事而异。

大凡热带民族都比较喜欢鲜艳缤纷的色彩，而北国人士则偏爱沉静素雅的颜色，当然，这与当地的环境气候与社会经济大有关联。金色，紫色，由于原料贵重，染制过程复杂，一向为皇族贵胄所喜。色彩的喜好，也会随着时代而变迁，倘若你有一天去法国游览，请看一看凡尔赛宫壁上法王路易十四的画像，除了那一身时髦的衣饰外，别忘了瞧瞧他那穿上红色高跟鞋，以丁字脚站立的模样！至于中国，《牡丹亭》中柳梦梅及《红楼梦》中贾宝玉代表的那身俊俏打扮，如今只能在戏曲中去寻找了。进入20世纪，色彩已在男性世界中销声匿迹，在正式的场合，除了黑、白、蓝、灰之外，还有什么色彩可以堂而皇之出现在男士身上？偶尔一抹红、紫、黄、绿，也只能瑟缩在一方丝巾及一条领带上了。但是，到了20世纪末，21世纪初，情况似乎在渐渐转化，各地爱美的男士，正在悄悄求变，释放自我，开始探索缤纷的彩色世界。

所有的色彩，既可带有正面的联想，也可引起负面的感觉，对于一位感性而敏锐的诗人，当然更是如此。布迈恪笔下的色彩，各有特性，可正可反，绿是"遍布世界的颜色／生灵万物的血液"，却可迷惑旁观者，使之恍惚蒙眬，或以"无比的不屑／睥睨着天地万物"；蓝是"鸟儿对天空／鱼儿对海洋"的纯洁之爱，然而却"满载回忆"、"带着巫术及魔法"、"充斥神秘与恐怖"；灰如愁雾，却又"至轻至柔"；银是哀悼的"泪之色"；雪是施于地下天上"白色的魔术"，白色虚无、真空、抹去一切；黄是"高与亮的精髓"；橙是"未熄的余烬"；铜为"秋叶之色"；棕却是"无谓之火的遗迹"；红能"尖叫"，也有"利爪"；粉红既是"肌肤之色"，也是"诱惑之色"；黑却最具威严，黑色之乡是"秘密之乡"、"潜危之邦"，那处永恒黑暗，子虚乌有。布迈恪的诗集，全书以《彩虹》始，以《玫瑰》终，外加一首特地为奥运而撰的《华光溢彩迎奥运》，乃形成了一个完整的《彩梦世界》。

翻译这本别具特色的《彩梦世界》，我采用的是尽量贴近原文的策略。在翻译过程中，传统所谓的"意译"、"直译"，近期热门所谓的"异化"、"归化"，根本不在念中。我所着意的是怎样与原诗相契相合，尽可能在原诗的格式（包括分行与无标点的特色），原诗的意境氛围，文字的节奏语感，整体的统一和谐各方面去用心揣摩。我所注重的是原诗的风格，这一系列乃超现实主义的现代英诗，诗中充斥着大量意象、明喻与暗喻，我力求把这种特色重现在译文中，非必要时，不予增删。全书共六十首诗，除了第一首之外，格式及分行全部与原诗相同。至于第一首《华光溢彩迎奥运》，为了使中译较易琅琅上口，我特意译成七言诗，共四行，一、二、四行押韵，这是与其余各首截然不同的尝试。

颜色词的翻译，向来是译者在双语转换的过程中，深感棘手的一个范畴。原因是颜色可分为基本颜色词与实物颜色词两种。实物颜色词是借一种实际存在之物，来指涉某种色彩，例如以翡翠（jade）来代表绿，以雪（snow）来代表白，然而因为各地环境的不同，文化的差异，一地的实物，未必存在于别处，因此中文里常见的豆沙色、蟹青色、菱色、藕色、米色等颜色词,就不宜也不易直译成英文,反之亦然。即使是基本颜色词,如红、黄、蓝、白、黑,在中外文化中,也会引起不同的联想,学翻译的人都知道,"嫉妒"一词,在中文里用"红色"表示,如"眼红";在英语里则用"绿色"表示,如"green-eyed monster",因此,译者处理时,往往会转"绿"为红,或易"红"为绿,做出相应的调整。

诗人布迈恪曾经说过:"我用一种色彩为形容词时,是为了它所表现的潜力,而不是为了它对一件实物的描绘。"他的思想,深受抽象派先驱康定斯基(Kandinsky)(1866-1944)及沃林格(Worringer)(1881-1965)的影响,他认为每一种颜色都拥有无穷的力量,正如每一个音符一般。这力量含蕴在指涉每一颜色的单词中,每当这单词跟其它字眼结合时,就会力量倍增,成为充满生命力的存在。诗人认为"极简抽象派的风格"(Minimalism),一旦运用到文学作品之中,"言简意赅"乃成为诗品的要诀。布迈恪曾经译过王维《辋川集》中的四十首诗,深受王维空灵清远诗风的影响,因此,下笔凝练精简,以简约的形式,来表达深邃的思想,就如大幅留白的中国画,落墨行笔处有诗,字里行间也有诗,诗人因此要求读者敞开心扉,充分领略诗中每一字、每一词的分量与涵义。

这本诗集原名Colours,而"Colours"既为"色彩",也有"旗帜"的意思,在此"华光溢彩北京聚"、"万邦竞相展彩旌"的时刻,诗集得以在北京由信誉卓著的商务印书馆出版,使我深感荣幸。

承蒙商务印书馆前总经理杨德炎先生、英语室主任周欣女士大力支持,黄国彬教授审校译稿,并提出宝贵意见,赖恬昌先生惠赐墨宝，为拙译赐题，特此致以衷心谢意。此外，本书的封面、插图都是布迈恪的作品，全书更附上布氏亲自朗诵的CD，弥足珍贵(由于第一首诗"华光溢彩迎奥运"乃诗人特地为奥运而作的新诗，故不包含在CD中)。

特别感谢的还有林青霞女士。与青霞相识相交以来，发觉我们虽然生活在不同的圈子，年龄也有一段差距，可是大家对文学、对艺术、对生命意义、对世间真情，却有十分投契的看法，因此会不时把晤谈心。承蒙她在百忙中为本书写序，使诗集倍添光彩。

记得2007年我们一起去探访季羡林教授时，两人不约而同都穿上色彩鲜艳的衣服，为的是给季老带上喜悦温暖的感觉。青霞那一身翠绿，是喜爱素色的她从来没有穿过的。颜色，除了表达个人的爱好与性情之外，原来也是一种巧思，一点慧心，一种对他人体贴与关怀的表现。

谨以此书，献给所有爱美爱梦的朋友，希望您在诗中找到喜悦，找到乐趣，从而营造自我独特的"彩梦世界"。

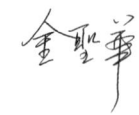

2008年1月17日

---

* 上述有关介绍原作者之部分内容，乃按照原序编译而成。

众彩缤纷

Olympic Colours

Five colours five rings
encircling the world
and bringing it to Beijing,
Beijing, for as long as the Games last,
capital of the planet,
where all the colours of the nations
will be unfurled

华光溢彩迎奥运

五色五环绕寰宇
华光溢彩北京聚
奥运期间地球都
万邦竞相展彩旆

Rainbow

The sounds of the colours
merge in a frenzied rhapsody
a passionate harmony
that rises
into an uncontrollable crescendo
beyond reach of reason

彩虹

众彩之声
汇成一阕疯癫的狂想曲
一片炽烈的和声
上扬至
失控的高潮
超越理性的范畴

绿色系列

Colours of the River

The blue sound of the fish
in the depths of the water
reaches me through a grey mist of gnats
as I sit on the bank of the river
joined by the soft whisper of the reeds

Birds speak in high yellow voices
disturbed by the red cry of a hawk

Drowned in this rising tide of colours
I drift into an indigo sleep

河流之色

河水深处
鱼儿的蓝音
穿越蠓蚋的灰雾达我耳际
正当我坐在水湄
与芦苇的喁喁细语为伴

众鸟以高亢的黄音交谈
受扰于鹰隼红色的鸣叫

沉溺于众彩喧腾的涨潮
我飘入湛蓝的睡梦

Colours of the Wood

The shadows between the trees
    are blue and grey
shot through with streaks of yellow
    cast by the sun

Patches of red black green
    flit among the branches
the birds of the wood

The colours of the wood
    merge in a manifold harmony of sound

On the dark lake
    the whiteness of a swan
rings out with the purity
    of a silver bell

森林之色

树隙的阴影
　　　蓝灰相间
丝丝黄晕自阳光投射
　　　穿插其中

抹抹红、黑与绿
　　　在枝桠间闪烁
林中的鸟儿

森林之色
　　　汇成万籁的谐音

在黑沉沉的湖上
　　　一只天鹅以纯白之色
发出银铃的
　　　纯净之声

Green 1

In its flow the river
gives off a green sound
that mingles
with the green scent of the water
to induce a trance
that transports the watcher
to a realm beyond time and space
ruled over by naiads
hidden behind a curtain
of hanging moss
waiting to pounce on the dazed intruder

绿之一

河川滔滔奔流
发出一声绿响
与流水的绿息相融
以引起一阵恍惚
将旁观者带入
超越时空的境界
那处由水仙统治
水仙藏匿
一帘垂苔的幕后
正等待着突袭迷茫的闯客

Green 2

Green enters me through every pore
the colour that pervades the world
the blood of everything that grows
filled with green I become one with the earth

绿之二

绿从我每一个毛孔渗入
遍布世界的颜色
生灵万物的血液
充盈着绿,我与大地合而为一

Green Shadows

Green shadows litter the floor
climb the walls
obscure the windows
mingle with the green leaves beyond the glass

Green mist trembles
on the edge of consciousness
as the waters of sleep rise
suffused with a glaucous light

绿影

绿影布满地板
攀上四壁
遮蔽窗扉
与窗外的绿叶相融为一

绿雾轻颤于
知觉的边缘
正当睡眠之泉涌升
弥漫着幽幽的绿光

Green Mist

Wandering over the paper
my pen
draws the outlines of a huge tree
a green glass ball hanging in space
a green eye
regarding the universe
with profound disdain

A green mist veils the stars—
a myriad gilded nipples

绿雾

游走于纸上
我的笔
绘出一棵巨树的轮廓
一枚玻璃绿球高悬天际
一只绿眼
以无比的不屑
睥睨着天地万物

一阵绿雾笼罩繁星——
无数涂金的乳头

Green Resonance

A green resonance echoes through the wood
the name Ching reverberates
like the clink of pebbles
rolling in a brook
or a silver bell
ringing in s darkened room

A green mist dims my vision
reducing the world
to an insubstantial dream
shot through with hints of black

The green pales
begins to change
till I am floating
in an ocean of blue

But the music of green
still echoes in my mind

Note: In Chinese the word ching, often used as a name, means "green." Strangely, it also means black, blue, and pale.

绿色共鸣

绿色共鸣于林中回响萦绕
青之名在震动激荡
如卵石轻击
滚动于清溪
或如银铃
叮当于暗室

一阵绿雾蒙眬了我的视线
将世界变成
一个缥缈的梦
束束黑色穿越其中

绿色转淡
开始变化
直至我飘浮于
蓝色的海洋

然而绿色的音乐
依然在我脑海萦绕回响

㊟ 中文里的"青"字,常用于名字,意谓"绿",然而出奇的青又可意谓黑、蓝及苍白。

Philodendron

Green hearts
poised in space
casting blue shadows
that move with the light

My heart goes out
to these green hearts
that draw their green blood
from the black earth

蔓

绿色的心
休栖于空中
投射出蓝影
随光而移动

我的心出迎
这些绿色的心
它们自黑土
汲取绿色的血液

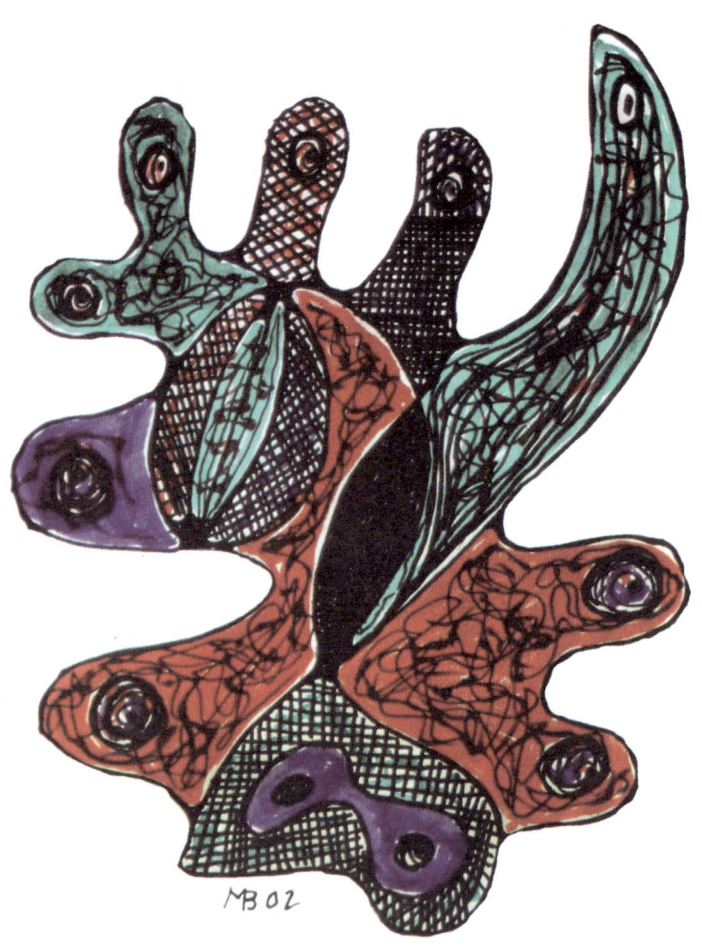

蓝色系列

Blue

Blue is the love of the bird for the sky
of the fish for the sea
the blue flower
the bride of night
wears a ring of blue stars on her finger

蓝

蓝是鸟儿对天空
鱼儿对海洋的爱
蓝色的花
夜之新娘
佩戴缀满蓝星的指环

Peacock Blue

Feathers shimmering in the sun
iridesce like moiré silk
rippling on the limbs of a dancer
who steps out of the light
into the shadows
of an enchanted wood
on a darkened stage
where mystery rules a world of magic
beneath a banner of peacock blue

孔雀蓝

羽毛在阳光中发亮
闪耀如水丝
于舞者肢体上泛起粼粼波光
舞者躁蹬出亮光
进入森然榭台上
一座着魔森林的阴影
那里，奥秘统治着魔术之乡
于一幅孔雀蓝的旗帜之下

Blue Evening

A blue evening begins to blossom all around me, casting indigo shadows that flutter like birdwings.

A yellow sound breaks the silence, high-pitched, shrill, standing out against the blue and indigo. It runs in veins of sound that spread through the blue tapestry of the evening.

The voices of the birds as they fall asleep on the branches are coral pink and dot the tapestry with tiny flowers.

A waterfall weaves silver threads.

蓝暮

蓝暮开始在我四周绽放,把靛蓝的影子四洒,如鸟翼掠动。

黄音打破沉寂,高亢,尖锐,在一片蓝与靛中突显。它在声脉中流淌,声脉于夜暮蓝色的挂幅中伸展。

众禽在枝桠间入睡之际,发出珊瑚红的啭鸣,百啭在挂幅上缀以朵朵小花。

一帘垂瀑织出银线丝丝。

Ultramarine

The ocean rolls in to the shore
carrying its colour
when it retreats
the beach is a brilliant blue
that pours into the soul and raises it
into the empyrean
the kingdom
of otherworldly birds
whose plumage is steeped
in the colours of the sea

佛青色

海洋带着色泽
滚涛拍岸
潮退时
沙滩一片艳蓝
倾注入灵魂,将之提升至
苍穹
天外之天
众禽的国度
禽羽饱含
大海的色泽

Prussian Blue

Waves of cold
    sweep across the landscape
to a background of music
    played on a flute of ice
by frozen fingers
    and frozen lips
birds shiver on the branches
    longing despairingly
for a splash of summer gold

普鲁士蓝

滚滚冷浪
扫过河山
来至音乐的背景
乐声由冻僵的手指
冻僵的嘴唇
以冰笛吹奏
鸟儿在枝桠上战栗
无望地期盼
一抹夏日的金黄

Indigo

Filled with the dark notes
of bass guitars
indigo's space is steeped
in deep longing
for the unattainable
the irrevocably lost
and echoes of vanished voices

靛蓝

充斥着低音吉他的
黑色音符
靛蓝的空间饱蕴
深深的憧憬
期盼那不可企及之梦
无以挽回之殒
以及消失之音的回响

Cobalt Blue

Hair streaming
the colour of the sky descends
settles on the walls
of a startled room
the background now
to mysteries and magic
where words and hands assume
the power of transformation
encircled by the colour of the sky
entangled in its streaming hair

钴蓝

发丝流泻
穹苍的色泽下降
降落栗室的
四壁
栗室已成为奥秘及魔法的
背景
那里,文字及众手掌控
蜕变的力量
由穹苍之色环绕
为流泻之发所缠

Pale Blue

Pale blue flows through my mind
wiping out everything
leaving only faint traces
to be deciphered by birds

浅蓝

浅蓝流过我心中
抹去一切
只剩下隐约的痕迹
留待鸟儿去辨识

紫色系列

Lilac

The purple scent of lilac
fills the leafy room
with the sounds of spring

紫丁香

紫丁香的紫芬
以新春之声
充盈叶茂的房间

Mauve

Mauve music purrs
silky and soft
carries the scent
of lavender and lilac
mauve floats above the earth
in a cloudy realm
laden with memories
holds out its hand
in a gesture of benediction

浅紫

浅紫之乐低声吟唱
轻柔温和
带着薰衣草及紫丁香的
芬芳
浅紫自地面浮升
飘于满载回忆的
云乡
以祝福之态
伸出玉手

Pale Mauve

Pale mauve surrounds me
dove colour
the colour of nostalgic music
filled with longing and the echo
of the irrecoverable past

淡紫

浅紫围绕着我
鸽之色
怀旧音乐之色
乐音充满依恋
和已逝往昔的回声

Purple

Plunging into purple
I meet all the loves of my life
floating in a magical darkness
distilled from the essence
of a thousand purple flowers

紫

纵身投入紫色
我遇见毕生的众爱
飘浮于
千朵紫花精髓
提炼而成的幽冥中

Purple Flower

A purple flower
    blossoms in the darkness
its scent is alive
    with sorcery and magic
a noble magic
    come from another world

The darkness in heavy
    and soft as velvet
wrapped in its perfume
    the flower turns slowly
back into the goddess
    it always was

紫花

一朵紫花
在幽黑中绽放
芬芳秘酵
带着巫术及魔法
由另一天地而来的
神秀魔法

幽黑沉甸
柔软如绒
裹于芬芳之中
紫花逐渐还原为女神
始终不变的前身

Night's Purple

Night's purple takes possession
like an irresistible river
sweeping all before it
washing all mundane visions
    from the eye

Forcing the mind to plunge
into its deepest recesses
into caverns filled
with mysteries and terror

where its greatest riches lie
out of reach of daytime's
pilfering fingers
into a purple darkness

that sways with the tide
flashing sometimes
when a shaft of moonlight
strays from its path

夜紫

夜紫统领
如一条滔滔奔腾的江流
扫荡一切
涤尽眼前
　　所有世俗的景象

强迫思绪投入
最深的溟蒙
投入充斥神秘与恐怖的
洞穴

那里,最丰盈的宝藏纷呈于
白日偷窃之指
无法企及之处
投入带紫的幽黑中

那幽黑随潮汐晃动
时而闪烁
当一束月光
在途中迷路

Purple Shadow

The shadow on the ceiling
is a purple fish
a shark
or a dolphin
leaping in the light
from a single lamp
seeking the ocean of darkness
the place of its birth

紫影

天花板上的影子是
一尾紫鱼
一条大鲨
或一只海豚
在一盏孤灯的
光芒中跃动
寻找黑暗的大洋
它那诞生之处

Purple Poppies

Purple poppies
flutter like butterflies
longing to break loose
from the tether of their stalks
and soar
into the enticing azure of the sky

紫罂粟

紫罂粟
翩跹如蝴蝶
冀希自茎链
挣脱
飞入
长空诱人的蔚蓝

Purple Petals Fall

Purple petals fall
on the still pool
the water weeps
for a vanished face
that will never again
be mirrored on its surface

The purple petals
float like music
in the silent air

紫瓣飘落

紫瓣飘落于
静止的湖上
湖水哭泣
为一张逝去的脸庞
那脸永不会再次
映照于湖面

紫瓣飘浮于
静谧的空中
宛如音乐

A Flood of Purple

A flood of purple sweeps me away
into a dream that devours me
like a flock of hook-beaked birds–

A gown of purple velvet
trimmed with yellow silk
purple grapes against a yellow moon–

Behind sulphurous clouds the moon hangs
like a golden gong waiting to be struck
with a hammer wrapped in purple cloth

紫潮

一阵紫潮
将我冲入梦境
梦境吞噬我,如钩喙的鸟群

一件紫绒镶黄丝的
袍子
紫葡萄衬映黄月亮

月儿在硫磺云后高悬
恰似一面金锣
等待紫衣裹住的锤子来敲响

Purple the Warrior

The warrior purple
enters the lists
bearing a burning lance
all other colours cower
cowed by purple's power

紫色战士

紫色战士
携带燃烧的长矛
开始战斗
一切颜色均自惭形秽
受屈于紫色的力量之下

紫红系列

Magenta 1

Magic flower
sorcerer of souls
a dream flower peering out
through a curtain of green leaves
a monstrous flower
whose brilliance dazzles the sun
magenta

紫红之一

神奇的花
灵魂的巫师
一朵梦花从一帘绿叶
向外窥视
一朵巨花
其华彩使日光晕眩
紫红之色

Magenta 2

Magenta has a song
    that differs from all others
sung in a deep cavern
    it echoes round the walls
issues from the mouth
    in the shape of a flock of birds
whose brilliant colour
    makes other birds seem pale

紫红之二

紫红色有首
　　　不同凡响的歌
唱诵于深穴
　　　在四壁回响
发自嘴唇
　　　以鸟群为形
其烂灿的华彩
　　　使众鸟黯然失色

Fuchsia

The colour of a heart
    burning with a dark fire
a lantern spreading the bloodlight
    of abandoned passion
the royal colour
    of the queen of the garden

洋红

心之色
　　　以炽火燃烧
一盏溅出弃爱
　　　血光的灯
园中之后的
　　　皇胄之色

银灰系列

Grey

Grey encircles me
a sorrowful mist
obscuring and restricting
confining me
within a melancholy cocoon
an illusory protection
from the dangers of delight

灰

灰环绕着我
一阵愁雾
阻挡万物、限制一切
将我囚禁于
忧郁的茧中
使我免遭欢愉之险的
虚幻保护

Dove Grey

The softest of music
mingled with the moving shadows
of leaves and flowers
and the pale scent
of fading lilac

鸽灰

至轻至柔的音乐
掺揉着花叶
婆娑的影子
及萎谢紫丁香的
淡淡幽香

Silver

A silver bell is pealing pealing
repeating a lamentation
a complaint
the sound is the colour of the bell
silvery—the colour of tears

银

银铃叮当不绝
重复着一声哀悼
一个抱怨
响声是铃的颜色
银——泪之色

Snow

White magic casts its spell
over earth and sky

White roses fall
their petals line the ground

Birds and bare branches
add touches of black

The white world has buried
    all colours
far out of sight

雪

白色魔术在地下天上
遍施魔法

白色玫瑰飘降
落瓣片片铺于地上

鸟与秃枝
添上黑色数抹

白色世界把众色埋葬
使之消匿不见

White

White presents itself to me
in the form of nothingness
as the essence of the void
as a lake in which all colours are drowned
as death that dissolves and wipes away
leaving a blank page
on which something is waiting to be written

白

白以虚无的形态
向我展现
如真空的精髓
如众色沉溺其中的湖泊
如消溶且抹去一切的死亡
剩余一页空白
尚有东西待写

黄色系列

Yellow 1

Yellow clangs with a clash of cymbals
echoes through all the corridors of the mind
sets the notes of a reed flute dancing
on the banks of a summer river
sings with the voice of a bird
flashing among the leaves of a dark forest
yellow—essence of high and bright

黄之一

黄以击钹之声铿锵作响
回声响彻心中的长廊
使芦笛的音符
在夏河之湄翩翩起舞
并以鸟之啭鸣歌唱
闪烁于黑林的叶丛中
黄——高与亮的精髓

Yellow 2

Yellow rings a plangent bell
sings in a high-pitched voice
that startles birds from their nests
shatters glass and turns silk curtains
inside out
laying bare the shadows
that lurk in the corners

黄之二

黄响着哀怨的铃声
以高亢之音歌唱
令鸟儿自巢中惊起
将玻璃震碎
丝帘翻转
使蜷缩屋隅的影子
暴露无遗

The Shadow of Yellow

The shadow of yellow
glides across the page
scattering splinters of amber
torn from a ring

Purple becomes one with the night
white flutters its wings
and feathers fall from the sky

Blue too descends from the sky
embracing everything

黄影

黄影
滑过纸页
洒下琥珀的碎片
撕裂自一枚指环

紫与夜合而为一
白掠动双翼
羽毛自穹苍纷纷落下

蓝亦自天而降
拥抱一切

Lemon Yellow

Sunlight passing through green leaves
falling on a dancing stream
the notes of a reed flute
mingled with birdsong
and a pair of plovers
rising startled from a field of hay

柠檬黄

阳光自绿叶隙间透入
降于舞动的溪流
芦笛的音符与
鸟鸣合奏
一双千鸟
自干草场受惊飞起

The Dream of Yellow

The dream of yellow
    becomes a curtain
that hides the darkness
    its birdsong voice
protects the ear
    from the sounds of suffering
the fear that the curtain will tear
    the birdsong fall silent
turns the blood to water
    the heart to ice
but the dream of yellow
    lingers in the memory

黄之梦

黄之梦
　　变为藏匿黑暗的
帷幔
　　其鸟啭之音
保护耳朵
　　免聆痛苦之声
因恐黄帷撕裂
　　鸟啭休止
令热血变水
　　心灵变冰
然黄之梦仍在回忆中
　　萦绕不散

Orange

Orange shows its teeth
in a wide white smile
whispers warm words
glows like a living ember
in the midst of green darkness

橙

橙露齿而笑
展示白牙
喁喁轻诉暖心的话
闪耀如未熄的余烬
于墨青之中

Copper

Copper kettle
    steeped in wood smoke
        and gypsy violins
Copper colour
    the colour of sunset
        and autumn leaves

铜

铜壶
　　饱含木烟
　　沉浸于吉卜赛小提琴声中
铜色
　　落日之颜
　　秋叶之色

Brown

Brown—the colour of autumn
but the autumn just before winter
not the autumn of scarlet leaves
interposes itself between my eyes
and the bright colours I seek
burnt umber the relic
of some pointless fire

棕色

棕——秋之色
是冬前之秋
而非红叶之秋
置身于我双眸与
所觅艳彩之间
烧赭土之色
无谓之火的遗迹

红色系列

Red 1

Red shrieks in my head
its talons claw at my brain
its ruby eyes
peer into places
meant never to be seen

红之一

红在我头颅里尖叫
以利爪抓住我的脑
它那红宝的眼睛
窥入
本来永不该瞥的地方

Red 2

The sound of pounding drums
the sound of pulsing blood
of the beating heart

Huge flowers with the perfume
of death and decay
glowing in the same dark forest
in which the birds
have torn the flesh
from the bones of a murdered poet

红之二

鸣鼓之声
跃动的心
血脉贲张之声

带有死亡与腐烂气息的
硕大之花
在黑林中闪耀
那里鸟儿
从遇害诗人的骸骨
撕下血肉

Pink 1

Pink—the colour of flesh
the colour of temptation-
flashes like sudden shafts of light
bursting through a grey mist
turning the world
into a garden of roses
whose scent echoes
like alluring music

粉红之一

粉红——肌肤之色
诱惑之色
烁亮如束束闪光
穿透一层灰雾
把世界变为
一座玫瑰之园
园中的气息回响
宛如诱人的音乐

Pink 2

The colour of the lost and longed for
of the vanished breast
of ballet shoes and faded roses
of seashells and falling petals
the colour of the ideal

粉红之二

失落与憧憬之色
萎缩乳房
芭蕾舞鞋与凋谢玫瑰
贝壳与落英之色
理想的色泽

Pink Doll

Hurled by a hidden hand
the pink doll
hurtles to earth
smashes in a hundred pieces

The fragments arrange themselves
in the shape of a heart
a pink heart
a broken heart

beyond hope of repair

粉红娃娃

由隐形之手抛出
粉红娃娃
摔在地上
裂成百块

碎片重新自组
拼成心形
一颗粉红心
一颗破碎心

复修无望

黑色系列

Black 1

Black widow
monster of power
queen of darkness
Venus of night
whose embrace is death
and everlasting bliss

黑之一

黑色的寡妇
力量的恶魔
黑暗之后
夜之维纳斯
其拥抱即死亡
及永恒的欢乐

Black 2

Black silk, black veil, black hat
the depths of decadence
the colour of seduction
of power and domination
of glad surrender
risen from the dark past

黑之二

黑丝、黑罩、黑帽
颓废深处
诱惑之颜色
力量与统领之色
从黑色往昔衍生的
自甘屈从之色

Black 3

Black hair black silk black gloves
black shadows

The Queen of Darkness
rules with an ebony rod

黑之三

黑发、黑丝、黑手套
黑色的影子

黑暗之后
以黑玉权杖统治天下

Black 4

Plunging into blackness
I enter the world of secrets
of hidden menace
of the threat of oblivion
of absorption
into everlasting darkness
and the state of non-being

黑之四

纵身跃入黑色
我进入秘密之乡
潜危之邦
受遗忘威胁的国土
及全神贯注的天地
投入永恒的黑暗
以及子虚乌有的境界

Black Dot

Lost on the edge
    of a spreading pool of purple
a black dot
    swims desperately to and fro
till a streak of yellow
    takes it by the hand
and leads it to the promised land
    where a golden beetle waits
to welcome it
    to the kingdom of colours
where the pale-blue air
    is as pure as springwater

黑点

失落在
　　　一滩紫液的边缘
一个黑点
　　　拼命往返泅渡
直至一条黄线
　　　伸手把它牵引
带往应许之地
　　　那处有只金色甲虫等候
迓迎它
　　　进入彩色王国
此中浅蓝的空气
　　　纯净一如春水

Black and Red

Black and red
blood and iron
a caste mark on the brow
a sword in the scabbard
the clash of weapons
the battle of the alcove

黑与红

黑与红
血与铁
眉上阶级的印记
鞘中的剑
武器的交锋
壁龛的战争

Black and Green

Peering into the dark pool
I see a face
ravaged by ripples
tangled in green reeds
criss-crossed by black waterbirds

Is it mine
yours or a stranger's?

黑与绿

窥进黑黝黝的池塘
我瞧见一张脸庞
给涟漪弄皱
受绿苇纠缠
让黑色水鸟穿梭划过

这脸是我的
你的,还是一个陌生人的?

Black and Purple

Deepest of the dark
richest of the rich
colour of dominion
royal sister of gold
the colour of iron
the colour of velvet
hand in hand
rulers of the earth

黑与紫

黑色之最黑
丰腴之最丰
统领之色
金色的皇妹
铁之色
绒之色
双双携手
共治大地

Black and Mauve

The dream drowns
in falling water
the word is buried
beneath black earth

From the black earth
springs a black flower
a black tulip
flower of mourning

Black notes
between black lines
spell a mauve music
that melts the heart

黑与浅紫

梦在垂泻之水中
淹浸遇溺
世界埋于
黑土之下

从黑土
萌生一株黑花
黑色的郁金香
举丧之花

黑色线条间的
黑色音符
吐出融心的
浅紫音乐

瑰色灿烂

The Colours of the Roses

All the roses have paled to white
drunk on their perfume
their colours have left them
on a mad search
for other homes

The snowballs of the viburnum
have turned pink
the lilies are stained with red

Yellow mauve red pink
all white flowers
have taken on a colour
stolen from the roses

Throwing the garden
into chaos and confusion

玫瑰之色

满园玫瑰褪为白色
沉醉于其芬芳
其色泽纷纷离去
拼命另觅
其它的家园

荚蒾树上的雪球
转为粉红
百合染上红晕

黄、紫、红、粉
所有白花
都染上一种窃自
玫瑰的色泽

使花园变得
乱纷纷，闹哄哄

作者简介
About the Author

MICHAEL BULLOCK was born in the UK in 1918, came to Canada on a Commonwealth Fellowship in 1968, joined the faculty of the Creative Writing Department at UBC in 1969, and retired as professor emeritus in 1983. He is the author of more than fifty works of poetry and fiction and two plays, as well as some two hundred translations of books and plays from German, French and Italian. His own work has been translated into many European and Eastern languages, especially Chinese, as well as Punjabi and Bengali. A selection of his poems in Chinese was published in 2000 in the series World Classics in Poetry of the 20th century. In the same year a Bengali translation of his surreal novella *Through the Veil of Maya* was published in the series Contemporary World Classics in Indian Languages. His *Selected Works 1936–1996*, edited by Peter Loeffler and Jack Stewart, appeared in 1998. This was followed by *Sonnet in Black and Other Poems* (1998) , *Erupting in Flowers* (1999) , *Nocturnes: poems of night* (2000) , *and Wings of the Black Swan: poems of love and loss* (2001) .

His work is the subject of a 340-page critical study by Jack Stewart: *The Incandescent Word: the Poetic Vision of Michael Bullock* (1990) . In April 2008 Michael Bullock celebrated his ninetieth birthday which was marked, among other things, by the publication of his book *Seasons: poems of the turning year*. This was followed later by his latest collection of poems *The Enchanted Garden*. In 2007 his poem *"Butterfly"* was displayed on the Shanghai-Metro alongside poems of William Wordsworth and William Blake to represent British poetry.

译者简介
金圣华教授小传

香港崇基学院英语系毕业，美国华盛顿大学硕士，法国巴黎大学博士；现任香港中文大学翻译学荣休讲座教授及香港翻译学会会长，中国翻译工作者协会理事及福建师范大学外国语学院客座教授。曾任香港中文大学校董及新亚书院校董，香港双语法例

咨询委员会委员。1990年—1992年出任香港翻译学会会长期间,曾筹办十项大型活动,筹募翻译基金,并创设香港首项翻译奖学金。1998年至2000年为香港中文大学筹办"第一届新纪元全球华文青年文学奖",2002年推出第二届,2005年则推出第三届,在世界各地华裔社会影响深远。金教授曾出版多本著作,如《英译中:英汉翻译概论》、《英语新辞词汇》、《桥畔闲眺》、《打开一扇门》、《一道清流》、《桥畔译谈:翻译散论八十篇》、《傅雷与他的世界》、《因难见巧:名家翻译经验谈》、《春来第一燕》、《认识翻译真面目》、《译道行》、《春燕再来时》、《荣誉的造象》、《江声浩荡话傅雷》、《三闻燕语声》、《齐向译道行》等;并翻译多部文学作品,如麦克勒丝的《小酒馆的悲歌》、康拉德的《海隅逐客》、厄戴克的《约翰•厄戴克小说选集》、布迈恪的《石与影》和《黑娃的故事》,以及傅雷英法文书信中译等。

金教授亦为《翻译学报》创刊主编。2004年应香港电台之邀出任"黄金书中寻"节目嘉宾主持,推介文学及翻译作品。1997年6月因对推动香港翻译工作贡献良多而获OBE(英帝国官佐)勋衔。

图书在版编目（CIP）数据

彩梦世界 （英汉对照）/〔加拿大〕布迈恪著；金圣华译.
北京：商务印书馆，2008
ISBN 978-7-100-05769-1

Ⅰ.彩… Ⅱ.①布… ②金… Ⅲ.①英语-汉语-对照读物 ②诗歌-作品集-英国-现代 Ⅳ.H319.4：I

中国版本图书馆CIP数据核字（2008）第022721号

所有权利保留
未经许可，不得以任何方式使用。

CĂI MÈNG SHÌ JIÈ
彩 梦 世 界
（英汉对照）

〔加拿大〕布迈恪/著　金圣华/译

商 务 印 书 馆 出 版
（北京王府井大街36号　邮政编码100710）
商 务 印 书 馆 发 行
北京中科印刷有限公司印刷
ISBN 978-7-100-05769-1

| 2008年6月第1版 | 开本 889×1194 1/32 |
| 2008年6月北京第1次印刷 | 印张 5 1/4 |

定价：35.00元